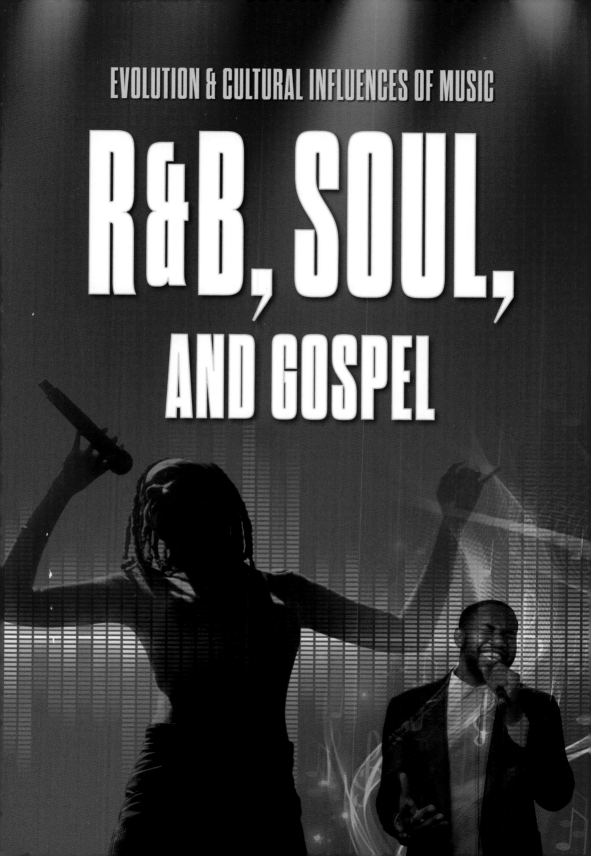

EVOLUTION & CULTURAL INFLUENCES OF MUSIC

R&B, SOUL,
AND GOSPEL

EVOLUTION & CULTURAL INFLUENCES OF MUSIC

COUNTRY
ELECTRONIC DANCE MUSIC (EDM)
HIP-HOP
LATIN AND CARIBBEAN
POP MUSIC
R&B, SOUL, AND GOSPEL
ROCK
STAGE AND SCREEN

EVOLUTION & CULTURAL INFLUENCES OF MUSIC

R&B, SOUL, AND GOSPEL

ERIC BENAC

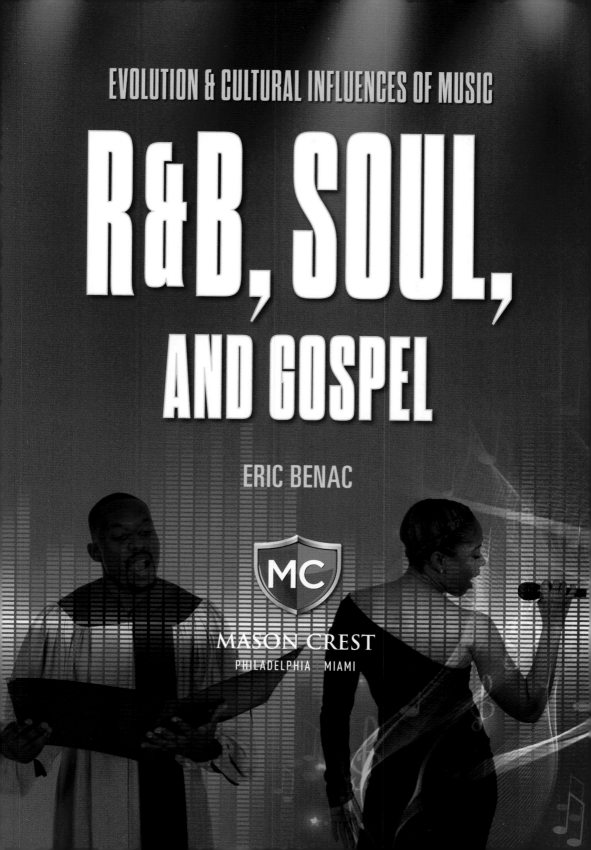

MC

MASON CREST
PHILADELPHIA | MIAMI

MASON CREST
450 Parkway Drive, Suite D, Broomall, Pennsylvania 19008
(866) MCP-BOOK (toll-free) • www.masoncrest.com

Printed and bound in the United States of America.

CPSIA Compliance Information: Batch #ECIM2019.
For further information, contact Mason Crest at 1-866-MCP-Book.

First printing

ISBN (hardback) 978-1-4222-4375-6
ISBN (series) 978-1-4222-4369-5
ISBN (ebook) 978-1-4222-7440-8

Library of Congress Cataloging-in-Publication Data on file at the Library of Congress.

Interior and cover design: Torque Advertising + Design
Production: Michelle Luke

Publisher's Note: Websites listed in this book were active at the time of publication. The publisher is not responsible for websites that have changed their address or discontinued operation since the date of publication. The publisher reviews and updates the websites each time the book is reprinted.

QR CODES AND LINKS TO THIRD-PARTY CONTENT

CONTENTS

KEY ICONS TO LOOK FOR:

Words to Understand: These words with their easy-to-understand definitions will increase the reader's understanding of the text while building vocabulary skills.

Sidebars: This boxed material within the main text allows readers to build knowledge, gain insights, explore possibilities, and broaden their perspectives by weaving together additional information to provide realistic and holistic perspectives.

Educational Videos: Readers can view videos by scanning our QR codes, providing them with additional educational content to supplement the text. Examples include news coverage, moments in history, speeches, iconic sports moments, and much more!

Text-Dependent Questions: These questions send the reader back to the text for more careful attention to the evidence presented there.

Research Projects: Readers are pointed toward areas of further inquiry connected to each chapter. Suggestions are provided for projects that encourage deeper research and analysis.

Series Glossary of Key Terms: This back-of-the-book glossary contains terminology used throughout this series. Words found here increase the reader's ability to read and comprehend higher-level books and articles in this field.

Kirk Franklin, pictured at the 2017 Soul Train Awards, is one of the biggest gospel music stars today.

WORDS TO UNDERSTAND

a cappella—music without instrumental accompaniment.

celebratory—feeling or expressing happiness and pride.

congregation—a group of people assembled for religious worship.

lyrical—expressing the writer's or musician's emotions in an imaginative and beautiful way.

multifaceted—having many facets or sides.

repertoire—a stock of pieces that a performer knows or is prepared to perform.

secular—denoting attitudes, activities, or other things that have no religious or spiritual basis.

streamlined—make something more efficient and effective by employing simpler designs.

CHAPTER 1

Introduction to Gospel, R&B, and Soul Music

Over the past century, popular music has gone through many trends, and new genres have formed out of a multitude of music and performing styles. An example is the way that gospel music—particularly the style sung by African-Americans throughout the nineteenth and twentieth centuries—helped to inspire modern performers as diverse as Kanye West and Adele.

Of course, these changes didn't happen overnight. They occurred as gospel music slowly turned into two parallel and related forms of music: R&B and soul music. These two genres are among the most popular and influential ever created, and their evolution has affected all of popular music. You can hear the complex vocal arrangements common in these genres in classic groups like The Beatles and even in boy bands like N'Sync. And the hard-driving rhythms of R&B and soul are all over hip-hop and dance music.

Gospel, R&B, and soul music have not remained static and unchanging. Every decade has brought new musical ideas, more skilled artists, and improved production and performing techniques. Each of these aspects helped to make soul and R&B into some of the most predominant music styles of today.

Gospel Music Origins

Anybody interested in R&B and soul needs to understand the massive influence that gospel music had on these burgeoning and steadily growing genres. Historians continually point to gospel music and its many offshoots as having a powerful influence on African-American music and genres beyond this subset of music stylization. The ecstatic singing and religious fervor common in the genre found inroads into soul, funk, R&B, and even early rock and roll.

Gospel music has a complicated history that extends far into the earliest days of American settlement into European Christianity and much farther back. The earliest form of gospel music was likely the intoning singing of ancient monks. This style is far removed from what most people consider gospel music but did set a basis for traditional Christian music and a tradition for singing during ceremonies that extends on to modern religious ceremonies.

The religious connections in gospel music are obvious and are a big part of its appeal to fans. Though the musical elements of gospel-styled music can be complex and **multifaceted**, successful gospel combines religious fervor and relative musical simplicity with performing excellence to create a genre that has influenced not just multiple styles but which has touched the lives of millions:

"Gospel Music is a shining beacon of hope, a fantastic journey of joy divine, and a triumphant victory in God that comes from deep down in the souls of God's Chosen People," notes the Gospel Music Heritage Month Foundation. "The greatest melodies and the most stimulating songs have been given to this Nation and the World through the African American experience."

Gospel music is predominately vocal-based music that focuses on massed voices singing either in unison or harmony.

Members of the choir perform at St. Peter's Catholic Church in Worcester, Massachusetts. Music has long been an important part of church services, and this is particularly true of predominantly black denominations like the African Methodist Episcopal (AME) Church or the Church of God in Christ.

Unison singing features the performers singing the same melody while harmonic singing utilizes complimentary themes to create chords or new rhythms in the music. The most basic form of gospel music focuses almost solely on vocals, though performers may clap their hands or stomp their feet to keep time and add a little extra dimension to the sound.

However, many modern gospel genres use instruments to add more melodic and harmonic content to the sound. The most basic instrumentation consists of a piano or an organ playing the chords for the melody. Other styles of gospel utilize rhythmic instruments, like tambourines and drums, and even bass and

Slaves work in a cotton field in South Carolina. The songs that slaves sang while working often had Christian themes, and were forerunners to today's gospel music.

electric guitar. This expanded instrumentation influenced a broad variety of musical forms and made gospel music, arguably, the most critical music style for African-American and general American pop music.

The Earliest Roots of Gospel

Gospel music can be broken down into two different sub-genres: that practiced by African-Americans and traditional Christian gospel music. The two styles are very different and should not be confused. While both genres will use similar lyrics and sing many of the same songs—including traditional hymns—the approach to the music varies massively.

Traditional Christian gospel music is nearly as old as the Christian faith and focuses on solemnly singing hymns and songs throughout the church and in various ceremonies. Harmony is sometimes not utilized in this style, which connects it to the chanting approach popular with ancient monks. The effect of this style of gospel is to create a worshipful and thoughtful atmosphere that almost hypnotizes the **congregation** into a state of communion with God.

African-American gospel music is focused not on chanting or solemnity but on celebrating faith exuberantly and excitingly. Singers were encouraged to put passion and excitement into their singing and to clap to the music to create a rhythmic pulse that made the ceremony more exciting and enthralling. Dancing and high levels of vocal harmony are also typical with this style, which makes a church ceremony a **celebratory** experience.

This tradition is one that has many roots throughout history. "Gospel music first emerged from the fusion of West African musical traditions, the experiences of slavery, Christian practices, and the hardships associated with life in the American South," notes an essay at the educational website Teach Rock. "Over time, as the influence of the African-American church grew and the Great Migration transported thousands of African Americans from the South to America's northern industrial cities, the influence of this musical genre expanded. Ultimately, Gospel's reach would extend well beyond the religious realm, directly affecting the world of **secular** music."

The direct African influence goes back to pre-slavery times and comes from religious celebrations and rites common on the continent. Many of these rituals—though they were by no means common to every element of the African experience—featured heavy drumming, passionate vocals, and wild dancing in an attempt to connect with the gods of African religion. The obvious parallel with African-American gospel makes it clear how important this style of music was on its expansion.

And, unfortunately, the experience of slaves during this period had an incalculable influence on this style of music. The demeaning and devastating impact that slavery had on generations of African-Americans is well documented, but many may not realize how much it influenced the formation of music on the continent. Most of this influence came when Christianity became prominent among slaves and later freed former slaves and the ways it mixed with their traditional African religion.

Black slaves attend a church service on a South Carolina plantation, 1856. Plantation owners encouraged their slaves to become Christians and taught them passages from the Bible about being obedient to their masters. Slaves, of course, preferred stories like Moses leading the Israelites out of bondage in Egypt.

As Christianity became prominent and the suffering of the race grew worse under the pressure of slavery, a style of music then known as the "negro spiritual" was born. These songs formed from the work song familiar on plantations—and which originated in African culture—but focused on spirituality and escaping from the bonds of slavery. This style profoundly influenced gospel music and transformed it into both a celebratory and mournful form.

The Influence of Revivals

Though gospel music arguably existed long before being defined, the first published use of the term was in 1874. In this year, Philip Bliss released a book called *Gospel Songs: A Choice Collection of Hymns and Tunes*. The songs collected here were designed to be sung in church and were a break with traditional church hymns, which were often hard for many amateur singers to perform.

The release of this book was concurrent with the rise of revival culture throughout the nation, particularly in the South. Revivals weren't uncommon in the country before this time

GOSPEL GENRES

Many offshoots of gospel music exist, many of which take on elements of other genres. For example, gospel blues integrates blues-based instrumentation into gospel music to celebrate religious dedication. Popular performers influenced many religious and secular performers.

Philip Bliss helped to popularize gospel music during the nineteenth century. He donated most of the money that he earned from these songs to Christian charities.

and typically focused on Methodist and Protestant churches. The first American revival took place in the 1730s and 1740s and was called the First Great Awakening. A revival focused on rebuilding a connection with God and Jesus and was fueled by a break between traditionalists in the church and those who wanted to modernize the religion to add new rituals and concepts of self-awareness. One of the biggest changes common during these revivals was a focus on gospel music that was easier to sing and which was simpler for the common person to understand. The revival movement of the late 1800s was started by Dwight L. Moody and the Holiness-Pentecostal movement. This church focused on using celebratory music—which was similar to the African-American gospel music of the time—and was designed to not only provide an outlet for religious energy but to entertain and enlighten listeners.

Many popular musicians originated during this time, such as Ira D. Sankey, arguably the most successful of the many gospel singers of the time. Sankey was originally working at a government position before he met Moody at a YMCA convention. After attending an evangelical meeting, Sankey was inspired to focus solely on his singing career and became known for his sonorous voice and his passionate renderings of various hymns.

Sankey also became a prolific writer of gospel music, producing "sacred songs" that were published throughout his lengthy career. Many of his songs are still performed today and include compositions such as "Room for Thee," "Tell the Glad Story Again!" "Tell Me the Story of Jesus," and "Jesus Knows Thy Sorrow." The words and music of these songs were deliberately simple to make them easier to remember and perform.

The success of Sankey has an influence on traditional gospel music still being felt today. Modern Christian singers often

Scan here for a short biography of modern gospel performer James Cleveland:

Known as the "Evangelist of Song," Ira Sankey was a popular gospel singer and hymn writer of the late nineteenth century.

use many of the same types of phrases and melodies utilized by Sankey, and many of the songs he published have titles that could be used by modern groups. Using Sankey as a basis, revival singers such as E.O. Excell, Charles Tindley, and Charlie Tillman popularized the form and spread it far beyond the South.

Though this style of gospel was not as influential on R&B and soul as African-American gospel, it does have an impact on the form. The simpler format and basic lyrics influenced the idea of chanted choruses and a call-and-response between lead singers and background singers common in much of soul. This concept started as the priest calling out lyrics in church to which the congregation would answer back, sometimes mirroring the lyrics but often expanding on them.

The Expansion of Gospel Music

During the early twentieth century, gospel music expanded and became famous around the nation. For example, the development of recorded music and the radio made music easier for people to consume. Instead of going to church or a revival to listen to a performer, people could listen to songs in the comfort of their own home. They could enjoy gospel music while relaxing, eating supper, or working around the house.

As a result, multiple performers started becoming very popular and expanding the form in various ways. These more modern performers also expanded their instrumentation and **streamlined** the style to make it more attractive to the average listener, including those with more limited religious interests.

Promoter, songwriter, and music professional James D. Vaughan took advantage of radio broadcasts to spread the popularity of gospel. He pressed records and delivered them to radio stations, ensuring that they got played. Vaughan also put together traveling quartets—each of which included four talented singers and a backing band—who performed on these recordings.

As artists got successful, he published songbooks of their songs. As a result, fans of gospel could perform their favorite tunes at home on a piano or in church. And as gospel expanded to include differing genres, backwoods singers, performers, and recording artists started integrating these styles into their repertoire. For example, the Carter Family—arguably the first country band of all time—started marketing their recordings as gospel music. They found huge success with their fans.

Another big influence on this radio success was the Holiness-Pentecostal movement. This religious movement utilized a form of gospel that was a simplification of the European style of African-American gospel music. The idea behind this style was to unite the congregation into a unified celebration while allowing them to perform and participate in whatever way that they saw fit. For example, participants were encouraged to bring in extra instrumentation, as long as they could play well.

This tradition helped to make gospel music more appealing to a broader range of people. Performers often brought in instruments such as tambourines, electric and acoustic guitars, saxophones, and other types of instruments to expand the available instrumentation of gospel music. Gone was the complete focus on either **a cappella** tunes or limited playing and in its place was a more exciting and diverse tradition that made gospel music diverse between one church and the next.

For example, jazz and even classical music started becoming an influence on the genre in many ways. Jazz's impact included the integration of ragtime piano playing, which brought an extra rhythmic element to the compositions and the genre. Classical made an impact with more detailed harmonies and detailed singing arrangements. For example, the Blind Boys of Alabama—who were still touring in the late 2010s—utilized intricate vocal harmonies that went well beyond traditional gospel music but which still celebrated God and other spiritual elements.

A.P. Carter (center), his wife Sara (right), and their sister-in-law Maybelle (left) had several hits performing as the Carter Family during the 1920s and 1930s. Some of their gospel songs would become country music standards, like "Keep on the Sunny Side" and "Can the Circle Be Unbroken?"

A Change Into Rock and Roll

The popularity of gospel music in the early part of the twentieth century spread far beyond the religious world and the African-American community. As this genre played on many radio stations and spread the word, as it were, a growing number of musicians embraced the style or expanded upon it in a variety of ways to make it more successful. "Over the next few decades, groups such as The Zion Harmonizers, from New Orleans,

Gospel music star Sister Rosetta Tharp was unconventional because she was not afraid to play her gospel music in regular nightclubs, which many Christians frowned upon. Her guitar-playing style influenced many early rock stars, including Johnny Cash, Elvis Presley, Little Richard, and Bob Dylan.

The Golden Gate Quartet, hailing from Norfolk, Virginia, and Nashville's Fairfield Four, cemented the style, traveling the South in buses, raising the roofs of churches and auditoriums throughout the chitlin' circuit in gospel battles that pitched one group against another in a show of one-upmanship that left audiences in tatters," writes music historian Paul McGuinness.

Gospel had become show business for many of its biggest performers and continued to change in many ways. One of the biggest changes was the integration of the electric guitar into the performances of Sister Rosetta Tharpe. This performer became very popular in the 1930s and 1940s by taking the fledgling electrical guitar and making it a celebratory tool for her performances. She also utilized heavily rhythmic backing to make her songs simultaneously more exuberant and catchy.

Her success integrating gospel with a rhythm and blues style made her one of the most popular singers of her time and an incredibly influential performer. Her guitar playing style was highly advanced for the time and unique. She drew upon blues and traditional gospel music in her guitar playing and fell upon a style that is, arguably, the first example of rock and roll. Chuck Berry—often called the Father of Rock and Roll Guitar—heavily copied her guitar playing and performing style.

This latter element of Tharpe's success was very influential on other early rockers. Tharpe was a very passionate and dedicated performer who wasn't above adding theatrical elements to her singing and playing. Viewers at the time found her mesmerizing and other performers took note of her impact on the audience. One of the biggest of these was likely Little Richard.

Born Richard Wayne Penniman, Little Richard was a dynamic early rock performer who focused heavily on rhythmic piano playing and wild vocals. Richard drew influence heavily from gospel music and later became a preacher. He utilized elements of call and response in his music and focused heavily on the same kind of simple lyrics and melodies common in gospel music at the time.

Other early rock stars influenced by Tharpe include Carl Perkins, Elvis Presley, Johnny Cash, and Jerry Lee Lewis. These performers took Tharpe's heavy rhythmic emphasis, **lyrical** guitar playing, and passionate singing and added their own unique touches. And while gospel music is undoubtedly a huge influence on rock and roll, it later transmuted to soul and R&B and became even more successful through these streamlined offshoots.

TEXT-DEPENDENT QUESTIONS

1. Why do gospel singers clap and stomp their feet?
2. How did revivals influence gospel music?
3. What gospel singer influenced rock and roll guitar playing with her unique performances?

RESEARCH PROJECT

Find several traditional hymns and a book of modern gospel lyrics and examine the similarities and differences between the approaches. What kind of phrases and language do both styles of music use? Are modern gospel lyrics easier for you to understand when compared to traditional hymns? Listen to recordings of each and compare the music. Which do you like more and why do you think that is the case?

James Brown's dynamic singing style and energetic stage presence helped make him one of the biggest music stars of the 1960s. Known as the "Godfather of Soul" for his importance to the genre, Brown also had a huge influence on the development of pop, hip-hop, funk, and other music genres.

 # WORDS TO UNDERSTAND

boogie-woogie—a style of blues played on the piano with a strong, fast beat.

crossover—the process of achieving success in a different field or style, especially in popular music.

bordello—a brothel or home of prostitutes.

integration—combining (one thing) with another so that they become a whole.

polyrhythms—a rhythm which makes use of two or more different rhythms simultaneously.

CHAPTER 2

Soul and R&B Start Taking Form

While gospel music remains a popular form of music even now, it gradually expanded and broke into more secular forms of music that remain popular even now: soul and R&B. And while the sounds of these genres have changed over the years, their influence is undeniable. For example, pop singers like Christina Aguilera and Katy Perry emulate soul singers of the past with their passionate vocals and expressive tones. And rap music is highly influenced by the rhythms of R&B.

The biggest differences over the years have been in instrumentation, outside influences, and mainstream acceptability. Early R&B and soul focused on live instrumentation that was often relatively simple, but upbeat and exciting. The singing was expressive and emotive and focused on romantic and personal topics. And most of its fans were African-American, though many artists of the time experienced some **crossover** success in the mainstream.

In modern times, however, these trends have heavily changed. The instrumentation in music influenced by soul and R&B is often synthetic and features programmed beats instead of real drummers. In rap music, in particular, the music is often highly sampled or electronic to create an update on the hard-driving, but basic, instrumentation of the early genre forbears.

And, just as importantly, mainstream acceptance of these genres is at an all-time high. In fact, rap music is currently the most popular style on the pop charts, which is something that would have been impossible in the early days of R&B and soul. This increased acceptance is as much a commentary on the progress culture has taken towards **integration** as much as it is a reflection of how soul and R&B helped fuel greater understanding.

"The music was very instrumental, and it helped the races connect during a time of bigotry and racism," notes songwriter Syl Johnson. "[White parents] wouldn't let the kids listen to the records [by black artists] … but they hid under the covers, listening to the songs on transistor radios, and when they grew up, bigotry disappeared. It's still here, but R&B and soul music was very, very instrumental in bridging racial gaps between black and white."

The Early Roots of Soul

Soul music was the logical evolution of gospel music that formed by integrating more secular blues music and lyrical themes with the form. Blues was a related type of music played primarily on the guitar, which had roots in African-American songwriting. Early blues music typically included simple melodies backed with soulful lyrics, complex guitar playing, and spirited singing.

Though he was far from the first artist to perform blues music, Robert Johnson was among the most influential of these artists. Johnson originated many unique guitar playing techniques, such as playing a moving bass line with his thumb, as well as several styles of slide playing. He played in many juke joints—bars or music performing venues—and on street corners to passersby. Unfortunately, he was murdered when he was twenty-seven by a jealous husband, so there are relatively few recordings of his music.

However, the work of Robert Johnson spread to other

The Crossroads in Clarksdale, Mississippi, marks the spot where, according to legend, musician Robert Johnson sold his soul to the devil in return for the ability to play the blues.

musicians such as Muddy Waters, B.B. King, and many other skilled blues players. The form was later fused with more jazz-oriented styles by artists such as Duke Ellington and Count Basie. Although neither performer could be called a "soul" musician, their unique combinations of blues, jazz, and gospel helped to influence its development.

Furthermore, the exact origin of soul music cannot be pinpointed to a singular artist. Though James Brown is often

Sculptor Andy Davis's revolving bronze statue of American singer Ray Charles is located in a plaza in Albany, Georgia's Riverfront Park.

called the Godfather of Soul, Brown had many contemporaries performing similar styles. However, Brown's popularity in the African-American community—and even the pop charts, at times—makes him a vital artist in the early development of the genre.

Brown was born into poverty and raised in a **bordello** and was self-taught on multiple instruments, including guitar, drums, and bass guitar. His earliest music focused on his intense vocals—based on gospel pleading—backed with upbeat and simple music. Though many of his songs are fine compositions, the performance of the music was typically more important than the notes played. And though his lyrics were often simple, his pleading tone made them feel more vibrant.

However, the Godfather of Soul's influence goes far beyond soul music. "Brown had both the message and the music to live up to that title," writes Henry Adaso. "But he also put the 'Good Foot' forward with a funky new sound that later became known to the world as 'hip-hop.' It's no coincidence that Mr. Brown is one of the most sampled artists in hip-hop…. His rhythmic innovations had a major influence on most popular music styles, including R & B, soul, funk, disco, rock 'n' roll and, of course, rap."

Though Brown did a lot to popularize soul, and fueled the development of funk and disco, he was far from the only artist to make soul a legitimate music form. Ray Charles—nicknamed the Genius—may have been the most important artist making soul. Charles' innovations lay in fusing gospel music with secular lyrics and more blues-based forms. Like Brown, Charles focused heavily on powerhouse vocals, though he had a more subdued and even thoughtful style by comparison.

Other important artists who influenced soul music include Otis Redding, Sam Cooke, and Etta James. James, in particular, was skilled at bringing a mournful tone to the music that connected it heavily to the African-American experience. Redding and Cooke later expanded the form to include even higher levels of gospel and even pop styles to make it more appealing to a wider audience. However, Jackie Wilson perhaps experienced the highest level of crossover success, particularly with songs like "Reet Petite."

Soul Expands in the 1960s

Though soul music had roots in the early and late 1950s, the form truly expanded and become successful during the 1960s. It was during this period that soul went beyond being "race" music—as it was termed at the time—to become more popular with all audiences. This moment is crucial for music history and has helped to fuel a higher level of integration over the years, including the increasing popularity of singers like Michael Jackson in the 1980s and the popularity of rap music.

During this time, though, African-American performers often ran up against high levels of discrimination. Many radio stations wouldn't play their songs or would only play them during specific blocks of time dedicated to "black" music. This segregation mirrored the racial struggles at the time, problems that much soul music alluded to with its potent and soulful sound.

Aretha Franklin's gospel roots flavored her most popular hits of the 1960s, including "(You Make Me Feel Like) a Natural Woman," "Respect," "Think," and "Chain of Fools." She became known as the "Queen of Soul."

Some of the most important aspects of this growth were increasing label interest in soul music. Music label Atlantic Records focused heavily on a variety of soul songs and attempted to break the music out into a pop format. Although a few singers—such as Ray Charles, James Brown, and Sam Cooke—had hits in a crossover vein, these were rare exceptions that only showcased the truth of musical segregation. Simply put, the hits by these artists were often streamlined versions of their sound that appealed to a broader base.

However, Atlantic Records was instrumental in promoting soul music during the 1960s, particularly with singers such as Solomon Burke. This performer performed classics such as "Cry to Me" and "Down in the Valley" that were successful in a more pop-oriented realm. And the surprising success of "Stand by Me" by Ben E. King also helped open the doors for more soul acceptance, including a boost in Aretha Franklin's career and the growth of African-American-oriented labels such as Stax and Motown.

Stax was located in Memphis, Tennessee and focused on simple, but driving, tunes that not only appealed to African-Americans but a broader pop audience. Hits such as "Green Onions" by Booker T and the MGs—the backing band on nearly every Stax recording—and "Soul Man" by Sam and Dave helped make Stax soul—an organ-dominated style—popular. And in Detroit, Motown was popularizing a broad array of artists and genres.

Motown took soul music and streamlined the sound into more pop-friendly styles and integrated more melodic content to create an incredibly successful label. Though the content of soul could be considered "watered down" by genre purists, the success of the label did much to integrate African-American music with the pop charts.

This expansion of the form helped to fuel sub-genres that took elements of soul and tweaked it a little. For example,

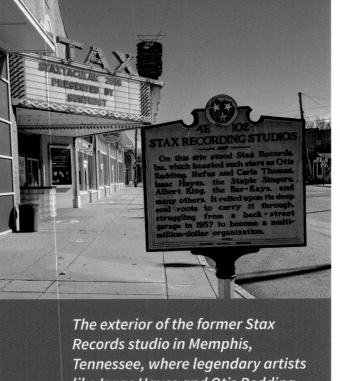

The exterior of the former Stax Records studio in Memphis, Tennessee, where legendary artists like Isaac Hayes and Otis Redding recorded soul and R&B hits. Today the building is home to a museum of American soul music.

James Brown increased the tempo of his music and focused strictly on rhythm to create funk music. Crossover artists like Sly and the Family Stone took funk music and fused it with rock and pop to achieve success. And performers like Marvin Gaye, Al Green, and Curtis Mayfield developed the form beyond its romantic basis and began performing politically conscious work that helped open the doors for the later agitation of rap music.

And as music technology improved, many soul artists expanded the form. Stevie Wonder integrated synthesizers, clavinets, and other high-tech instruments into his style to create a funk and soul form that was unique to him. Future performers, such as Prince, would draw upon this electronic style and expand it even further in decades to come.

Rhythm and Blues Makes an Impact

The development of rhythm and blues—or R&B—music began around the same time as soul and ran concurrently with its changes. The two styles continually influenced each other to expand upon the basic style in a variety of ways. R&B focused heavily on simpler versions of blues and jazz to create a style of dance music that was heavily popular in African-American clubs of the 1950s.

QUEEN OF SOUL

Aretha Franklin was one of the most important and influential soul performers of all time. Her early music drew upon gospel music and emulated the intensity of the style with her heavy and impressive vocals. Franklin was skilled at integrating pop music into her songs and wasn't afraid to make political statements with songs such as "Respect." Her influence was strong in the genre until she passed away in 2018.

For example, Louis Jordan took **boogie-woogie** rhythms and tied them to blues melodies and relatively simple instrumentation to create a gritty style that was very popular in its time. In 1948 alone, Jordan had three songs in the top five at the same time. Jordan's innovations were taken up by others around the same time and became one of the most prominent in the genre.

For example, artists such as Big Joe Turner and Billy Wright expanded on the style in various ways by adding saxophones and other instruments to the sound. The lyrics often focused on simple topics, such as love and having a good time, and featured chanted choruses and call-and-response backing vocals. These touches came from gospel and blues but were simplified to make the music more memorable.

The popularity of this form forced the *Billboard* charts to replace the term "Harlem Hit Parade"—an antiquated idea even at the time—with "Rhythm and Blues" in 1949. The popularity of the genre increased as artists continued to push the boundaries of acceptability. For example, Paul Williams released the chart-topping song "The Huckle-Buck" in 1949, a tune that stayed number one for nearly a year.

Though tame by today's standards, the track featured suggestive lyrics that alluded to sex. The dance associated with the tune also became controversial because it required the dancers to move their hips in a slightly suggestive matter. Such songs came to be known as dirty boogies and triggered wild reactions in concert. On more than one occasion, dirty boogies caused concerts to be shut down by promoters and venue owners, which only increased the popularity of the style.

It was during this time that African and Cuban music started influencing R&B more heavily. These changes included emphasizing the backbeat to make songs easier to dance to and catchier. However, some of these rhythmic influences were surprisingly complex and often made the music richer in harmony and meter.

For example, styles such as *tresillo* expanded beyond the ragtime and cakewalk rhythms of the style to provide more diversity. Jelly Roll Morton was particularly critical in this fusion, as he continually added new rhythmic elements to his music. For example, he often utilized hand clapping and foot stomping into his tunes, which drew heavily upon traditional African music. These innovations expanded R&B far beyond its simpler styles and later fueled the development of more complex jazz.

"Morton learned to play piano at age 10, and within a few years he was playing in the red-light district bordellos, where he earned the nickname 'Jelly Roll,'" notes a biography of the performer. "Blending the styles of ragtime and minstrelsy with dance rhythms, he was at the forefront of a movement that would soon be known as 'jazz.'"

Other important innovations in R&B at the time included increased instrumental combinations—including a string bass, electric guitars, and baritone sax—that made the sound fuller

To see how soul and R&B songs are written, scan here:

and more impressive. An expansion from simple one-time rhythms to more complex "stomp" patterns also originated during this time. While primitive compared to the **polyrhythms** of later R&B and funk music, this first step helped to open up the form.

Expansion of the Form in the 1950s and 1960s

As R&B expanded in popularity throughout the 1950s and 1960s, the form changed slightly in various ways. For example, hits such as "Double Crossing Blues" and "Cupid's Boogie" by Johnny Otis became synonymous with the sound of the time. However, groups started performing in different styles that expanded beyond Otis's basic R&B sound to integrate more expansive sounds and motifs.

For example, a cappella groups started popping up to produce a variety of hits. These included the Clovers, a vocal trio who combined blues and gospel to create a unique sound. This style would become increasingly popular and was often either streamlined or simplified to make it more appealing to broader listeners. Just as importantly, more radio stations started playing this music.

Mahalia Jackson was one of the most popular gospel singers from the 1940s until the early 1970s. She was very active in the Civil Rights Movement, working with Martin Luther King, Jr. and others to protest against segregation and discrimination.

The biggest early break was likely in 1951 when DJ Alan Freed out of Ohio started "The Moondog Rock Roll House Party" on WJW. Sponsored by Fred Mintz—who owned an R&B record store—this show not only opened up listeners to more African-American music—albeit late at night—but also influenced the development of future music as Freed called this music "rock and roll."

And this was the era when Little Richards, Elvis Presley, Jerry Lee Lewis, and Fats Domino took on this style and helped to fuel the early rise of rock and roll. This style simplified R&B even further and often featured white performers—though not always—performing covers of songs written and performed by African-American performers.

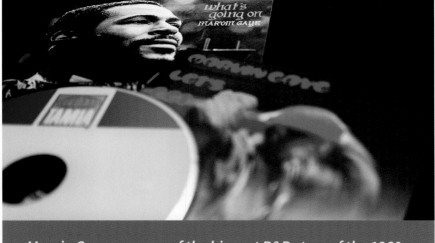

Marvin Gaye was one of the biggest R&B stars of the 1960s and 1970s. His 1971 album What's Going On? is considered one of the greatest records in music history.

For example, Elvis' "Hound Dog" was originally sung by African-American singer Big Mama Thornton as "Hound Dog Blues." Thornton's single version sold between 500,000 and 750,000 copies: Elvis' sold nearly 10 million. Such issues were not uncommon in the rock and roll world at the time and were very frustrating for the many African-American performers who vied for much-deserved success.

However, traditional R&B still existed alongside rock and roll and took a slightly different tact. Ray Charles got his first big crossover success in 1955 with "I Got a Woman" while The Chords' "Sh-Boom" in 1954 became the first substantial R&B crossover charting hit. And Bo Diddley combined rock with R&B stomp rhythms to create an intriguing crossover sound that became increasingly popular.

Stax and Motown increased in popularity during this time as well and spanned well into the 1960s. R&B artists were now fusing more pop elements into their music in an attempt to get more success. For example, "Chain Gang" by Sam Cooke had a pop-based rhythm that made it a success in 1960. And many successful soul artists (like James Brown and Stevie Wonder) began integrating R&B styles into their sound, further mixing the genres and creating a potent blend that would fuel innovations in the 1970s and 1980s.

During the 1960s Diana Ross was the lead singer of The Supremes, the most successful group in Motown's history. After leaving the group in 1970, she began a successful solo career in the 1970s and 1980s.

TEXT-DEPENDENT QUESTIONS

1. What R&B song featured mildly suggestive lyrics that caused clubs to be closed down when played?
2. Which soul and funk artist inspired hip-hop music with his rhythms?
3. Who was the Queen of Soul?

RESEARCH PROJECT

Study the concept of polyrhythms and talk to a music teacher about how these rhythms appear in R&B and soul music. Listen to examples of these rhythms from music at the time and listen to modern music inspired by R&B and soul. Do you hear these rhythms in modern pop songs or have they disappeared? Why do you think that they are/are not present? Write up a brief explanation of this issue.

The historic Motown Records building is located in Detroit, Michigan. Motown was one of the most successful R&B/soul record labels, and played an important role in bringing black American performers into the mainstream.

WORDS TO UNDERSTAND

cinematic—connected to or emulating films and movies.
contemporary—belonging to or occurring in the present.
psychedelic—a dense style of rock music heavily influenced by drug use.
schmaltzy—cheesy or overly emotional in an unbelievably way.
simultaneously—occurring at the same time.

CHAPTER 3

The Challenge and Changes of the 1970s and 1980s

The 1970s were a unique time in the pop music world. The trends of the 1960s, which had emphasized experimentation and expansion, were reversed in the 1970s. Instead of growing towards something greater, most artists tried to consolidate their gains and to expand upon already existing styles. While there are those who bucked this trend, in general music in the 1970s became slicker and easier for casual fans to digest.

And this trend was common in the R&B and soul genres. The once harder-edged and blues-influenced sound was becoming more and more pop-oriented. Gospel influences, while still present in a few small ways, were mostly disappearing. A lot of soul and R&B focused on entertainment in the 1970s, as bands and singers sanded the difficult elements of their music away and became more successful.

However, some artists worked against this change, with some success. For example, the integration of synthesizers, more machine-like beats, and ambitious songwriting concepts helped to add diversity to the genre. These artists often took advantage of the advanced recording techniques to create sounds that would have been impossible a decade earlier. Gone were the

Improvements in recording studio technology enabled the production of more complex R&B and soul songs during the 1970s.

days of bands playing a song live in the studio: now, groups could record their parts separately and on different days.

Although these changes helped to make soul and R&B more successful in the 1970s—particularly offshoots like quiet storm and disco—the louder and sometimes harsher sounds of the genre had been successfully mixed with pop styles. As a result, the genre started to lose some of its focus and became more about getting hits than innovating or making a statement about African-American culture.

As a result, these two genres entered and exited the 1980s in a very strange spot. Synthesizers and drum machines had taken over the instrumentation and made most **contemporary** soul and R&B practically indistinguishable from pop music. The popularity of both genres, therefore, waned slightly and many long-time artists struggled. And by the time the 1990s rolled around, both genres would be in danger of disappearing forever.

Soul Becomes Slicker in the 1970s

Advances in recording technology influenced some of the biggest changes in the recording industry. For example, studios expanded beyond two- and four-track recording options to include 12-, 24-, and even 48-tracks. This had a big impact on the genre because it allowed more instrumental layers, more fine-tuned control over the sound of an album, and a decreased reliance on overdubbing.

Track number indicates the number of recordings playing **simultaneously** on a record. For example, a two-track recording device has two, which means artists were typically limited to adding voices on one track and the instruments on another. Early examples of this style include Beatles recordings. In this era, microphone positioning and clear performances were essential because no repairs could be made if a performer made a mistake while playing.

While four-track and even eight-track recorders helped to alleviate this problem, the expanding ambition of recording artists often made overdubs necessary. For example, a typical four-track recording session may allow one track for the vocals, one for the guitars, one for the bass, and another for the drums. Any extra parts, such as strings, would have to be overdubbed on the backing track.

Overdubs required placing another recording on top of the tape and syncing it up with the recording. This was a laborious task and took engineers a lot of time to finish. Even worse, overdubs tended to muddy up the sound of a recording and make it less clear. The fact that so many great soul records of the 1950s and 1960s have great sound is a testament to the talent of the performers and the skill of producers and engineers.

However, expanding track counts made it possible for every instrument in a band to have its own track. As a result, a mistake by one performer wouldn't require endless retakes to fix: the

SOUTHERN SOUL

Southern soul was a sub-genre of 1960s and 1970s soul that originated in the Memphis region. Producers and artists who performed in this style took the passionate vocals from gospel and paired them with high-energy rhythms and thick horn arrangements to create a great new sound. Issac Hayes was one of the most important songwriters and arrangers in this genre. The impact of southern soul can still be heard in many rap music genres, particularly the rich southern sound of groups like Outkast.

performer would simply have to record their part again, rather than the whole band. Just as importantly, overdubbing was no longer as necessary, which helped create a smoother and cleaner sound.

As a result, recording artists like The Staple Singers and Al Green could integrate strings, expanded rhythm sections, and more onto their recordings to achieve a clear and efficient sound. The result was that R&B got a smoother and less jagged sound than past recordings. Just as importantly, many artists at the time started streamlining even further to achieve more success.

For example, Motown moved its studio to Los Angeles and begin producing a more pop-friendly sound that emphasized smoother soul and a softer style. Though some artists on the label—like Marvin Gaye, Michael Jackson, and Stevie Wonder—pursued slighter harder sounds after the move, even these artists occasionally played slightly **schmaltzy** music, such as Jackson's recording of "Ben."

George Clinton and the P-funk All-Stars perform at a music festival.

Psychedelic Music Adds Its Influence

While some mainstream soul started to become smoother and less hard-hitting, other artists integrated elements of **psychedelic** rock into their sound. For example, Sly and the Family Stone used heavy guitar and fuzz bass to create a dense and more atmospheric sound, particularly on albums like *There's a Riot Goin' On*. James Brown continued to push towards harder edges sounds and, by the 1970s, pursued a minimalist style that layered polyrhythms on top of simple vocals.

This funk breakthrough was expanded upon by more outrageous groups like Parliament and Funkadelic. Led by George Clinton, these two groups integrated even more expanded polyrhythms, dense keyboard and horn charts, and elements of harsh psychedelic rock into their sound. Funkadelic, in particular, had a rock-oriented sound and produced several concept albums that explored a sci-fi style, some social satire, and even elements of comedy. These bands' shows became legendary for their

Singer and songwriter Stevie Wonder was signed by Motown Records when he was just eleven years old. Innovative albums like Music of My Mind *(1972),* Innervisions *(1976),* Songs in the Key of Life *(1976), and* Hotter than July *(1980) made him one of the biggest music stars of the 1970s and 1980s.*

wild imagery and lengthy improvisations. Members of both groups often performed together with Clinton under the name Parliament-Funkadelic or the P-funk All-Stars.

Around the same time, groups like War and Earth, Wind, and Fire were attempting to mine several different genres at the same time. For example, War was capable of playing dirty funk like "Low Rider," pure pop like "Why Can't We Be Friends?" and more subdued balladry. Earth, Wind, and Fire took R&B to new levels of musical sophistication by blending rich vocal harmonies with skilled musicianship and ambitious songwriting. Both groups charted highly not just in R&B listings but in pop as well.

Meanwhile, Stevie Wonder continued to expand on the stylistics of funk and soul in surprising ways. For example, he started mirroring classical melodies and forms in his music, particularly on songs like "Village Ghetto Land" and "Pastime Paradise." Wonder—along with Marvin Gaye—attempted to showcase the plight of the African-American, though both had time for less serious music.

For example, Gaye followed up his classic protest album *What's Going On* (1971) with the sensual *Let's Get It On* (1973). The infamous opening riff of that song has become a part of pop culture legend and showcased Gaye's increasing interest in expanding the boundaries of sex-oriented material and what the radio would tolerate. This style influenced later boundary-pushers, such as Prince.

Similarly, James Brown started to focus heavily on similar subjects. His spoken-word track "King Heroin" detailed the dangers of drug abuse and its impact on the African-American community. Other tracks, like "Say It Loud, I'm Black and I'm Proud," featured simple chants that inspired dancers and showed a community-minded focus that was common throughout Brown's career.

Quiet Storm Fuels 1980s Soul

Although these groups remained popular throughout the 1970s and even into the 1980s, soul started to become a less prominent music form. The long-term success of the television show *Soul Train*, which aired from 1971 until 2006, did so much to keep the form alive. However, soul started to separate from R&B in upcoming years by smoothing the rough edges even further and creating a sub-genre known as quiet storm that became the predominant form of soul for years.

Quiet storm arguably originated in 1976, when Melvin Lindsey—then a radio station DJ at Howard University—started playing older romantic songs by African-American artists.

Lindsey found that these songs were among the most beautiful in the genre and wanted to share them with the world. Interestingly, this show caught on with a very large population of people— including an audience that was estimated 40 percent white and 40 percent black— and showcased the potent crossover success of this new radio format.

The "Quiet Storm" radio format—named after a 1975 Smokey Robinson album—started to influence musicians who were interested not only in the genre but in financial success. The style is highlighted by a smoother and lighter sound that has a slight jazz-influence. The tempos were usually quite slow, giving listeners time to enjoy the vocals. The melodies were also soft and the whole genre had a very relaxed, but somewhat romantic, feel that appealed to many.

Artists who pursued this style included Smokey Robinson— who always loved good ballads—singer Chaka Kahn, and former Sly and the Family Stone bassist Larry Graham. Even funk bands that typically pursued a harder direction typically added a few quiet storm moments on their album. This style became the predominant soul sound throughout the late 1970s, into the 1980s,

Smokey Robinson's 1975 solo album A Quiet Storm *was one of his most critically acclaimed recordings, and helped to inspire the "quiet storm" subgenre of R&B/soul music.*

Scan here to learn how to overdub musical performances:

and even up through the early 1990s. Many labeled this style "contemporary R&B," though it had more in common with soul.

R&B Becomes Smoother and Sophisticated

The same studio innovations that helped make soul smoother also affected R&B in a variety of ways. However, this smoother style also came with a surprising increase in sophistication. Beyond Stevie Wonder's experiments with synthesizers and classical and jazz music, Curtis Mayfield was expanding the narrative drive of R&B and creating a nearly **cinematic** sound that captured the minds of millions.

Though already a successful artist with R&B group The Impressions, Mayfield went solo and eventually produced the hit album *Super Fly*. Though nominally a soundtrack to a blaxploitation film, the detailed lyrics, sophisticated songwriting, and expert playing made the album a big success. Mayfield told

The rhythms of R&B were simplified to create disco music, one of the most popular styles from the mid-1970s to the early 1980s. Donna Summer became known as the "Queen of Disco" thanks to hits like "Last Dance," "Hot Stuff," and "Bad Girls."

detailed stories about crime on the streets and tried to educate his audience as much as possible. This increasing sophistication brought more critical notice to the genre.

Another example of this sophistication is Marvin Gaye's *Here, My Dear*. This 1978 double album started as a toss-off written as a divorce settlement from his wife. After the two divorced, Gaye agreed that the profits from his next album would go to her. Upset about the breakup, he initially considered knocking off an inferior product that would produce no hits, and therefore not provide his ex-wife with much money. Gaye dismissed this idea, and instead decided to use the project to explore the nature of their relationship and the effects of divorce.

The advanced songwriting, production, and lyrics on the album were beyond anything Gaye had earlier attempted. The songs lacked traditional verses and choruses but had fluid and ever-changing structures that progressed in a logical fashion. Gaye layered on many instruments, including detailed synthesizers, and elongated many of the songs to explore the nature of his divorce. And the lyrics were hard-hitting and emotional, as Gaye put the blame not only on his wife but on himself and attempted to understand what had gone wrong with their relationship. Although initially not a critical success, *Here, My Dear* is now considered one of Gaye's finest recordings.

This type of complexity and sophistication did not last, though, as funk transitioned to disco in the late years of the decade. Disco started as a sub-genre of funk that featured more expansive arrangements and simpler beats. Popular artists, such as Donna Summer, explored many variations on this sound, including electronic production. The success of the 1978 film *Saturday Night Fever* and its soundtrack brought disco to its highest mainstream appeal. However, a fierce fan backlash against the style later occurred. This triggered a difficult transition period during the early 1980s when R&B and soul both went into a quiet storm direction or were otherwise confused and without direction.

One-Man R&B Revolution

Although it is fair to say that harder-hitting R&B sounds weren't as popular in the 1980s as they were in the 1960s and 1970s, there are some exceptions. For example, Prince Rodgers Nelson was a one-man revolution who took the genre out of the staid past and helped to inspire a bold new future for the genre. New R&B artists still draw upon his 1980s and 1990s work for inspiration.

Prince was a multi-instrumentalist who wrote, arranged, performed, and produced nearly every one of his more than twenty albums. And his skill on these instruments was huge—band members often stated that if they were unable to perform a part,

Prince was an incredibly talented singer, songwriter, musician, and actor.

Prince would embarrass them by taking their instrument and recording it for them. This type of virtuosity was unheard of at the time and made him a thrilling performer.

Prince was also a sterling singer and a brilliant songwriter who fused genres as diverse as soul, R&B, funk, new wave, rock, country, jazz, classical, and electronic dance music into a rich blend. The release of the 1984 album *Purple Rain*, along with a film of the same title, made him an international star. Prince remained very popular and sold millions of albums until his untimely death in 2016.

During these years, he continued to try new forms and experimented wildly. And while there were moments where his reach exceeded his grasp, Prince was still able to make amazing music that could serve as an inspiration for future performers.

TEXT-DEPENDENT QUESTIONS

1. What production technique was eliminated by the addition of more recording tracks?
2. Who recorded *Here, My Dear*?
3. What R&B variation became very popular with the *Saturday Night Fever* soundtrack?

RESEARCH PROJECT

Examine various modern music styles influenced by disco and trace what elements unite them. For example, disco is known for utilizing a very specific beat that uses hi-hat cymbals in a specific way. Have you heard this rhythm in modern music before? Why do you think that beat is so popular? Discuss modern bands that use disco and describe how they tweak it for contemporary listeners.

Mariah Carey greets fans before a performance. The talented singer—known for her rare five-octave vocal range—dominated R&B/soul music in the 1990s and early 2000s, selling more than 200 million albums.

 # WORDS TO UNDERSTAND

antiquated—old-fashioned or outdated.
braggadocio—boastful or arrogant behavior.
dexterous—showing or having high skills.
insipid—bland or uninspiring.
preeminent—surpassing all others; very distinguished in some way.
relevant—closely connected or appropriate to what is being done or considered.
sea change—a profound or notable transformation.

CHAPTER 4

Soul and R&B Transform in the 1990s

By the 1990s, soul and R&B were in a state of decline. Artists still produced music in these styles, and many were still very popular. Michael Jackson continued to mine a pop-based R&B sound to remain one of the most successful recording artists of all time. His sister, Janet, was also exploring pop-based R&B and soul and creating music that didn't quite match her brother's in popularity but which wasn't too far behind.

Soul continued its trend of smoothness into increasingly low-key styles. Quiet storm lasted throughout most of the 1980s and stayed trendy, for a brief period, in the 1990s. The format had expanded well beyond the primarily African-American-oriented market to include a broader array of artists and focuses. For example, white singer Rick Astley was very popular during this period and had soul-oriented vocals as strong as nearly any African-American performer at the time.

However, all art is cyclical and the success of these styles would soon be limited by young new artists reacting against these styles. Typically, a pop music cycle takes ten to fifteen years to finish, though this cycle is increasing in speed with modern times. For example, a new style of music will come out that is innovative and which changes the approach of the entire

The tunes of white musicians who played R&B-style music became known as "blue-eyed soul." Among these artists was the duo Hall and Oates, who had many hits in the 1970s and 1980s.

industry. New artists innovate great styles while older artists switch over to these styles to avoid sounding **antiquated**.

As the style expands and changes, too many new artists dilute its impact or simplify the approach to make it less effective. Newer artists who were once inspired by this music may now find it **insipid** and want more high-energy or harder-hitting music to replace it. As a result, they start creating new music that captures the attention of a younger audience and which becomes more popular. This cycle happens constantly in the pop world, which is why it remains so fascinating to study.

And the cycle of 1970s and 1980s R&B and soul was starting to end by the early 1990s and would soon be replaced by a glut of new musicians pioneering new sounds. Rap started to become more

ELECTRONIC MUSIC

Electronic music was once seen as an experimental style that would never catch on in the pop world. Early proponents of this style, such as Edgard Varèse, were classical composers who used sound generators and oscillators to create music. Inventor Robert Moog helped to introduce electronic sounds into the mainstream by inventing a playable synthesizer. And later inventions, such as the Fairlight Emulator, made it possible for performers and producers to create parts without musicians. These innovations are still utilized in the genre today.

popular, though was nowhere near as mainstream as it would eventually become. Soul fled from the quiet storm sound and tried to regain more energy and passion. Changes in production—including an ever-increasing reliance on both programming and live instrumentation—continued to change styles forever.

Each of these new styles would remain popular throughout the 1990s and would help take R&B and soul into a new dimension. However, the 2000s would also bring in new styles that reacted to and against the trends of the 1990s. Many of these new writing and production methods would attempt to further regain the grittiness and passion of soul and R&B, including revival acts who sounded eerily similar to the artists who had inspired them to perform.

Rap Takes Over From R&B

Traditional R&B either disappeared in the 1990s or homogenized to become focused on more synthetic sounds and beats. For example, singers like R. Kelly and Usher brought an element of sex and groove back to the music but also utilized quiet storm or ballad arrangements from time to time. Female singers, like Janet Jackson, brought back a slightly harder edge to some of the music. However, R&B musicians at this time often did not write their own music or lyrics, similar to the old Motown or Stax production methods.

Although older or milder fans enjoyed this type of R&B, younger fans were mostly bored with the style. They couldn't relate to the smoother styles of most groups at the time and wanted something harder-edged that captured their angst and anger. This fact was particularly true of young African-American teens who struggled to fit into a society that shunned them.

As a result, rap started to take over the scene in a variety of ways. By the 1990s, rap was by no means new music. Early rap songs included novelty hits like "Rapper's Delight" (1979), which was over ten minutes long, and the socially conscious track "The Message," by Grandmaster Flash and the Furious Five. Rap during this period utilized mostly live instrumentation and a funk style to produce its grooves. However, more underground artists started producing new and experimental styles in the early 1980s.

This period is often called the Golden Age of hip hop or rap and lasted from the 1980s to the early 1990s. Artists during this period were creating new styles almost every day and using samples to produce their beats. For example, rapper Schooly D was known for a basic sound that focused on a drum machine and a turntable as he told detailed and often gritty stories of his time on the streets.

Other groups used samples to create a kaleidoscopic sound that often had more to do with psychedelic music than funk.

For example, De La Soul's debut album embraced a nearly "hippie" philosophy while creating layered and melodic music out of dozens of samples. A similar approach was taken by the Dust Brothers, a production group who produced albums by Beastie Boys that constantly changed due to the many samples utilized. Unfortunately, this golden age came to an end when stricter sampling laws were passed in the early 1990s.

And a newer age of harsher and more realistic rap music was on the rise with artists like Public Enemy, Ice-T, and NWA breaking from the pop-oriented rap of groups like Run-DMC and MC Hammer. These groups used dense production tracks and realistic stories of crime on the street to connect with youths experiencing these issues in their world. Unfortunately, some teens did not take the message—crime does not pay—and were inspired to a criminal lifestyle by some rap.

As the 1990s progressed and new styles were born, rap changed appropriately with the times. For example, artists like Ice Cube started integrating more electronic-styled productions to compensate for the increased difficulty of finding appropriate

Luther Vandross was one of the most successful R&B singers of the 1990s and 2000s, with hits like "Never Too Much," "Here and Now," and "Power of Love/Love Power." He won eight Grammy Awards, including four for Best Male R&B Vocal Performance.

music samples. And other musicians started integrating live instrumentation into their sound, instead, to make their music more organic.

A Tribe Called Quest is one group who tapped into these styles in a fresh way. This group focused heavily on jazz-oriented sounds and instrumentation and on the quirky vocals of rappers Q-Tip and Phife Dog. This style, known as alternative rap, broke away from the gangster-oriented styles of the time and integrated more unique storytelling methods.

In particular, Q-Tip was known as "The Abstract" for his ability to create strange rhythms that sometimes focused more on the sound of the words than the meaning. Similarly, The Wu-Tang Clan broke away from gangster **braggadocio** to focus strictly on the quality of their wordplay. Their debut album *Enter the Wu-Tang (36 Chambers)* introduced the world to nine incredibly talented rappers, including the RZA, the GZA, Raekwon, Ghostface Killah, and Method Man.

Each of these rappers would pursue lengthy solo careers that helped change the face of rap. For example, primary producer RZA eventually started to integrate sped-up soul samples—one of the first to do so—and to add live instrumentation to later records. The GZA focused mostly on his low-key, but literary, style to dazzle listeners with his wordplay. Method Man later paired with rapper Redman to create a series of fun and **dexterous** releases. And Raekwon and Ghostface Killah created expansive concept albums that told extended stories.

Their more cerebral approach was popular with many fans but other producers went for a simpler and more pop-oriented approach. For example, producer Dr. Dre expanded beyond the sample-based approach of NWA to add full bands to his recordings. His production style shifted to allow for more input from his musicians. Typically, Dr. Dre would program a drum machine beat and ask his musicians to improvise around the style. If he heard a beat or a riff that he liked, he would ask the musician to play it and would build tracks in this piecemeal way.

Dre also broke from the gangster-oriented style of NWA to discuss more personal issues, particularly with his debut *The Chronic*. This album—and the many others produced by Dr. Dre during this period—utilized a specific synthesizer tone to create hooks while layered bass, drum, and piano parts created a rhythmic backing. Dre's lyrics—which were written by other rappers—focused heavily on drug use, romantic problems, and other personal issues.

During the late 1980s and 1990s, Janet Jackson emerged from the shadow of her superstar older brother Michael to become a star in her own right. Janet blended R&B with hip-hop and dance sounds on hit singles like "Nasty," "Control," "Let's Wait Awhile," and "Rhythm Nation," all of which reached the top five on both Billboard's R&B and pop music charts.

Scan here to learn how rappers write their lyrics:

This approach proved popular and helped to start a sub-genre entitled G-Funk. Though Dre did not originate this form—DJ Quick was utilizing many of the same sounds on his debut album *Quik is the Name* in 1991, several years before Dre—the success of *The Chronic* made the sound **preeminent** in the mid to late 1990s. Other musicians who utilized this style included Eazy-E—another former NWA member—Warren G, Nate Dogg, and Tupac Shakur.

One group that used this style, Bone Thugs n Harmony, also utilized soul-based vocal arrangements to expand on the style even further. Though they were skilled rappers, they could also sing well and created many intriguing combinations with this style. But, like any genre, the popularity of G-Funk started to fade as listeners moved on to new things.

Dr. Dre himself helped to kill G-Funk by his release of *The Chronic 2000*. This solo album used more electronic elements mixed with more live playing in a way that sounded fresher and more alive than G-Funk. Rappers such as Eminem tapped into Dre for this style to become incredibly successful in the late 1990s. The innovations of this area often tapped into the rhythms and sounds of R&B and helped to keep the style alive in the popular consciousness.

Neo-Soul Revitalizes the Genre

Soul as a genre was in a state of confusion when the 1990s rolled around. The quiet storm revolution was still in effect and artists like Luther Vandross made a career out of soft melodies paired with loving lyrics. However, the style was no longer appealing to younger listeners, who considered the romantic sentiments of Vandross and others to be "cheesy."

In reaction to this change, new artists started to try to bring back the passion and vitality of old-school soul. However, the composition sophistication and production excellence highlighted by quiet storm weren't to be ignored or entirely forgotten. There was no going back to the simple four-track recording method of the 1960s and a full live sound. Instead, new soul artists would tap into as many inspiration sources as possible to create a new soul sound: neo-soul.

For example, many neo-soul groups were respected for fusing genres

Rapper and music producer Dr. Dre (Andre Young) shows off the Legend Award he received at the 2000 Radio Music Awards. Albums Dre produced, including his own The Chronic *(1992), Snoop Dogg's solo debut* Doggystyle *(1993), and Warren G's* Regulate...G-Funk Era *(1994) helped to establish the G-Funk sound of hip-hop music.*

such as jazz, funk, rap, electronic, world music, and more into a potent blend that made quiet storm seem calm and sedate by comparison. While quiet storm remained popular with its many fans, younger soul listeners were inspired and intrigued by neo-soul and flocked to it in droves. This period could be considered something of a Silver Age for soul because of the high level of innovation and creativity common among its performers.

Many of its top performers were female, which was unique among soul and R&B music at the time. Singers and rappers like Lauryn Hill and Erykah Badu were equally skilled in luxurious ballads filled with live instrumentation and in denser, hard-hitting rap-style productions. Hill, in particular, was popular due to her success with rap group Fugees, who had a surprise crossover hit with their cover of "Killing Me Softly."

Singer Erykah Badu at the 1998 Soul Train Music Awards, where she won four awards, including Artist of the Year. She is sometimes called the "Queen of Neo-soul."

The Fugees are a particularly interesting group during this period because they synthesized rap, soul, Caribbean music, and much more into a potent blend that appealed to many listeners. Producers/rappers Wyclef Jean and Pras Michel worked with Hill to create this sound before they broke apart into successful solo careers. Hill's *The Miseducation of Lauryn Hill* (1998) was easily the most popular and acclaimed of these releases and seemed to signal a new era of female singers and songwriters.

However, male performers were common during this period as well, including the original neo-soul performer D'Angelo. His debut album *Brown Sugar* was almost an entirely solo-driven affair. D'Angelo wrote much of the music, did almost all of the production, arranged all the music, and performed nearly most of the album on his own including piano, organ, guitar, bass, drums, percussion, and saxophone, though guest musicians do appear.

Hailed as a young genius, D'Angelo sold around half a million copies of the album, which was very strong for a first-time recording artist. After a five-year wait, he released his second album, *Voodoo*, which was even more successful. D'Angelo integrated more live instrumentation from a larger band to create a funkier and looser style. Selling nearly two million copies in the US alone, it positioned him as a key player in the genre. However, drug problems and personal issues kept him from recording until 2014, when his *Black Messiah* was released to heavy fanfare.

Another popular performer in this genre was Maxwell, who fused many similar influences into a coherent whole. Though he was not as acclaimed or as commercially successful as D'Angelo, Maxwell was more productive and has maintained a steady presence on the neo-soul scene. His music focuses heavily on live instrumentation and love thematics, which makes it very similar to the average neo-soul performer at the time.

However, this focus on old-school soul and trying to capture the spark that lit these older groups led to some confusion among many fans. As the genre eventually started to lose some steam in the late 1990s and early 2000s, many wondered about the impact of the genre. "Neo-soul, and some would argue hip-hop soul, never truly found a definition or a sonic boundary to differentiate them from other genres of music during their rise in the 1990s," writes Marcus Shepard.

Other music critics have made the same point over the years. The separation between neo-soul and contemporary R&B, for example, was often quite small. Some argued that the two genres didn't exist separately at all but were simply one extension of

African-American music. In spite of this confusion, neo-soul brought in new artists who helped keep the genre alive and **relevant** in difficult times.

And, in spite of its lack of popularity into the 2000s, it helped to set up a potential for increased popularity in the future. The 2010s have seen an increase in soul-based music, particularly that which sounds as close as possible to older styles. These trends are something worth examining later because they showcase the potential future of the form and how breakthroughs could continue to keep soul relevant.

Traditional Styles Suffered

Although the innovations of the 1990s made soul and R&B bold and exciting again, older artists and labels suffered. Although Motown survived into the 1990s and is still producing music, they continued to focus mostly on low-key music and quiet storm. Though they later adapted with the times and added harder-hitting artists to their lineup, their popularity was never the same compared to their 1960s and 1970s heyday.

And even incredibly popular artists like Michael Jackson and Smokey Robinson had difficulties in this era. While Jackson released his very popular *Dangerous* album during this time, he had to adapt his music to include harsher hip-hop-oriented styles. And 1980s pioneers like Prince also had to adapt to the times, often with limited success. This struggle made it very difficult for some performers to remain active and adaptable.

Meanwhile, singers like Smokey Robinson released music that mirrored, but did not match, their most popular styles. This difficulty was not uncommon even in the pop world but was particularly hard on R&B and soul performers because youth and vitality are so important for the style. However, Robinson and others still performed and sold records to their fans, in spite of **sea changes** in style.

TEXT-DEPENDENT QUESTIONS

1. What neo-soul artist recorded his debut *Brown Sugar* almost entirely by himself?

2. What rap group used samples to create a psychedelic style?

3. Why did the quiet storm R&B style lose popularity?

RESEARCH PROJECT

Examine the album sales of various neo-soul artists and see how they changed as the genre waxed and waned. For example, why do you think D'Angelo sold nearly two million copies of his second album but much less on his third? Could saturation have been a problem with this genre or do you think that the style didn't stand out, as many critics have claimed? Listen to a few recordings and try to identify the traits that stand out the most to you.

Whitney Houston performs in New York's Central Park, September 2009. The daughter of gospel and soul singer Cissy Houston, Whitney became a pop music superstar during the 1980s and 1990s, landing eleven #1 hits on the Hot 100 chart. However, she also has the distinction of recording the best-selling gospel album of all time—the soundtrack to her 1996 film *The Preacher's Wife*.

WORDS TO UNDERSTAND

emulate—try to sound like something or someone else.

entrepreneur—a business person who invests money in a variety of companies.

grittiness—a toughness, in music, defined by hard playing and edgy themes.

obscurity—being unknown or not talked about.

CHAPTER 5

Changes in the Twenty-First Century

The 2000s and 2010s were years of rebound and growth for R&B and soul. A surprising resurgence in traditional-sounding soul helped create new careers for high-quality performers and songwriters. Likewise, a new focus on contemporary R&B and an expansion of rap—still an essential offshoot of these genres—continue to push this music into bold and exciting new directions.

That's not to say that there haven't been some issues or moments of retreat. Rap and R&B both lost some popularity in the mid-2000s for a variety of reasons that will be examined. And traditional R&B is still most common in more underground circles, though some contemporary pop groups continue to play the kind of sharper and harder-edged R&B that helped to start the genre almost 100 years ago.

An increased emphasis on electronic music does tend to take some of the performance edges off of the music. However, this type of production also gives artists more freedom to create unique sounds and the chance to expand their style in a multitude of ways. As a result, many artists during this period start layering unique sounds in ways that were impossible in the heyday of soul and R&B.

And many of these artists continued to draw influence from rap and hip hop to cement the connection between the genres forever. Once low-key singers or performers started integrating more massive rap-style beats into their sound to stay relevant and vital. Others tried to remain true to their original music and either found success with their old fans or struggled to maintain their once high level of popularity.

British Soul Makes a Comeback

Although neo-soul dipped in popularity and nearly faded into **obscurity** by the beginning of the 2000s, soul music was by no means dead. However, the focus on the genre slowly changed from fusion—which artists like D'Angelo and Lauryn Hill had pioneered in their music—and more on creating a soul style that reflected the initial popularity and stylistic hallmarks of the form.

For example, new soul music would try to **emulate** the basic sound familiar on Stax, Motown, and other popular recordings but focusing on higher-quality production. Unlike in the 1970s, when production improvements robbed the music of some energy and **grittiness**, the new focus was on regaining the punch and passion that made classic soul so memorable.

This movement started in Great Britain, particularly England, where soul had always been a favorite genre. Artists such as Tom Jones and Dusty Springfield became very popular in the 1960s and remained successful in subsequent decades. The Foundations was a multi-racial group that focused on a Motown-inspired sound to create a uniquely British spin on the genre. They often used very detailed arrangements and dense vocal harmonies to create an effective pop-styled soul sound that captured the attention of many listeners.

Most soul musicians in Britain during this time were Caucasian, rather than African. The reasons for this vary and are mostly due to cultural differences in England and America. For example, many African-English performers were more interested in blues or reggae than they were in soul music. As a result, the handful of soul performers from England at the time were rarely African.

Amy Winehouse's hit song "Rehab" was meant to be a rallying cry that proclaimed her independence from drugs and alcohol. After Winehouse's death from a drug overdose, many fans saw the song as a cry for help from a tortured soul.

The same fact was true in subsequent decades, as David Bowie and Elton John experimented with soul, funk, and R&B in their music, sometimes with mixed success. Elton John's "Philadelphia Freedom" remains a classic of the genre while "Fame" by Bowie is a successful emulation of the funk of the time. Other artists attempting these styles struggled to nail them accurately.

But the 1970s did see some British disco—which took on elements of soul music and R&B—including from producer Biddu. This unique figure was responsible for such disco hits as "Kung Fu Fighting" among many others. A few other successful soul and R&B acts came from England at the time, but most of their music imports were pop or rock in the 1970s.

The 1980s and 1990s saw a substantial increase in soul music in England, including from a variety of white and black artists. Junior was a success at the time with hits such as "Mama Used to Say," a hit that made him the first English-African act to appear on the TV show *Soul Train*. However, most performers of British soul remained caucasian. Rock veterans, such as Phil Collins, turned to soul with covers such as "You Can't Hurry Love" while pop act Eurythmics tried out soul with songs like "Sisters are Doing It For Themselves."

Although many of these acts remained popular in the 1990s British soul scene, it wasn't until the mid-2000s that the genre truly exploded. It was during this time that a multitude of female singers started achieving crossover success by combining traditional soul sounds with modern production techniques. One of the biggest of these was Amy Winehouse, a respected singer and songwriter who unfortunately passed away due to alcohol and drug abuse.

Winehouse was singled out as the finest of these many performers due to her incredible vocal range, her reliance on high-quality musicianship, and her tortured lyrics. "You Know I'm No Good" detailed how troubled she was and told her lover not to expect her to get any better while "Rehab" mocked people who claimed that she needed help for drug addiction. Winehouse's success peaked in 2008 when she received five Grammy Awards, the most any British female artist has ever won in a single year.

Unfortunately, her tortured lyrics revealed a troubled psychology that caused her to become common tabloid fodder. Pictures of a wild-looking Winehouse appeared in American and British newspapers. Her partying had gotten out of control, and the tabloid pictures showcased the effect it was having on her body. Her teeth were starting to rot and fall out, and she looked 10 years older than she was before she passed away. However, her inspiration helped more soul-oriented singers gain the spotlight, even as they changed the form in subtle ways.

For example, Florence Welch—singer and songwriter for Florence + the Machine—took many elements of British soul and combined them with a more art- and punk-oriented approach to create a unique sound. Welch varies heavily from the traditional soul sound offered by other female British singers by integrating thicker arrangements filled with keyboards, guitars, and shifting harmonic vocal beds. Her lyrics are typically more mysterious and poetic and her sound grander and almost classic in its expanse.

By contrast, singer Adele's sound is typically a bit more humble than Welch's and emulates the traditional forms of soul and R&B. Her 2011 album *21* showcased a powerhouse performer

Janelle Monáe's 2018 album Dirty Computer *was praised by music critics.*

Jamiroquai helped to fuel much of the success of the British soul scene in the 1990s and early 2000s. Led by singer Jay Kay, they synthesized elements of funk, jazz, soul, R&B, disco, and hip hop into a danceable and articulate whole. While their peak was likely in 1999, when their song "Canned Heat" was famously used in the film *Napoleon Dynamite*, they have produced eight albums and still regularly tour.

who would perform on multiple instruments and write catchy songs in traditional styles. However, her follow-up album *25* proved that she could also create high-quality pop music, helping her sell millions of albums and to become the face of the British soul movement in many ways.

However, other singers, such as Joss Stone, Jessie J, Leona Lewis, Jay Sean, and Taio Cruz saw success and continue to remain relevant in the genre well into the 2010s. Though none have been as successful as Adele or as acclaimed as Winehouse, they remain stalwarts of the genre. Whether they will withstand the test of time remains to be seen, however.

Contemporary R&B Also Becomes Popular

During the 1980s and 1990s, a genre known as "contemporary R&B" increased and decreased in popularity throughout the years. This style featured more upbeat music than quiet storm but not quite as adventurous as rap or other types of underground variations on the form. For those who wanted

Usher is one of the best-selling R&B singers of all time. His 2004 album **Confessions** sold over 20 million copies and included four #1 singles.

a genre that fit comfortably in the middle of these two extremes, contemporary R&B was a good compromise. However, artists would become popular and disappear as audience interest changed or new artists debuted who took on the styles of past groups but expanded upon them.

For example, groups like Boyz II Men and Babyface had an R&B sound that focused on rich vocals and romantic lyrics to create a style with a broad appeal. Though rap did make an influence on the genre at points, contemporary R&B often focused mostly on synthesized sounds to craft a distinctive aura. For example, Mariah Carey debuted on this scene with "Vision of Love," a number-one hit that showcased a powerhouse vocalist backed by low-key music.

Whitney Houston also reached new peaks of popularity during this period, including her soundtrack to the 1992 film *The Bodyguard*. This album sold over 40 million copies, helping to fuel increased interest in contemporary R&B. Janet Jackson's 1993 album simply entitled *Janet* sold over 20 million copies and produced six top-10 hits. Other groups, such as TLC, fueled interest in this genre and helped it break out in a significant way among many listeners.

However, the increasing emphasis on rap music and changing trends found artists like Toni Braxton losing some record sales, though they continued to appeal to a core of dedicated fans. Part of this problem was due to saturation of the market while another may have been due to the format of the style itself. "Modern R&B isn't about discrete songs," explained music critic Robert Christgau. "It's about texture, mood, feel— vocal and instrumental and rhythmic, articulated as they're smooshed together."

Simply put, many fans started to feel like there weren't many differences between these artists and were fatigued with the style. As fans flocked to rap and other forms of music, contemporary R&B struggled to remain relevant. Artists still released albums, and many even sold well, but the peak of their popularity had passed. And when contemporary R&B became once again popular, many of these artists were supplanted by newer performers with more sophisticated styles.

One of the few old-school contemporary R&B acts to remain relevant in the early 2000s was Usher. Long heralded for his smooth voice, excellent songwriting, and skilled production, Usher released *Confessions* in 2004, an album that sold over one million copies in its first week and over 20 million copies worldwide. Usher was smart enough to update his sound with a subtle and sophisticated touch, bringing in slight hip hop influences to bridge the gap between generations.

Other successful contemporary R&B artists of the time followed suit. For example, Alicia Keys mixed her classically trained piano playing with her excellent voice and a variety of different genres. Keys could play seductive and romantic piano

To see a professional program drum beats, scan here:

ballads and stomp through hip-hop inspired backing tracks with equal ease. Her success helped to set the backdrop for a new glut of female singers in the genre, including Christina Aguilera jumping into the genre from her former pop style.

And Beyoncé Knowles broke free of girl group Destiny's Child to create a more adult and more style with her solo career. Her 2003 debut *Dangerously in Love* sold over five million copies in the United States alone and earned five Grammy Awards the same year. Beyonce was smart enough to find good producers who could push her into a dance-oriented direction without sacrificing her audience. This success helped fuel a career that stays strong and influential.

All of this interest in contemporary R&B likely peaked in 2004, when African-American artists recorded all 12 number one hits on the *Billboard* Hot 100. A full 80 percent of the R&B hits were recorded by African-American musicians, which was by far the highest at that point. The integration of R&B music with pop culture started in the early twentieth century was complete.

Genre and race boundaries seemed to no longer matter to the average listener.

And as the genre continued to expand, more and more electronic elements started to make their way into the style. The 2010s were, in particular, rich with artists embracing new trends. Auto-tune made its way into the genre, which was both celebrated and mocked. The excessive use of this tone-correcting instrument turned some listeners off of the style, as some believed that any singer who needed correction like that was probably not very skilled. Though auto-tune had been used in the past by artists like Cher, singer T-Pain popularized and perfected its use.

In spite of the backlash from some listeners, an increasing number of musicians continued to embrace electronic sounds in an attempt to update R&B even further. While electronic keyboards are nothing new to R&B—digital synthesizers were used in the 1980s and also in the 1990s—the sounds being made now are beyond what the more primitive instruments could achieve. Futuristic sound effects, full digital funk productions, and layered sounds move beyond even what a 48-track recorder offered in the 1970s. Simply put: a producer on a computer has an almost unlimited number of instrument combinations at their fingertips.

Rap Remains Prevalent

The commercial success of rap in the 1990s continued throughout the 2000s, representing younger fans interest in R&B music. However, rap underwent some strange changes during this period that may have influenced its popularity in many ways. The decade started strongly with Eminem releasing commercially and critically successful albums produced by Dr. Dre. The rapper 50 Cent also released a successful Dre-produced album, *Get Rich or Die Trying*, which showcased crime-oriented lyrics over the top of typical Dre production.

However, pop music started taking influences from hip hop in a way that caused the genre to begin losing a little steam. For example, many pop singers, like Justin Timberlake, asked hip hop producers to provide beats for their music. This heavy influence of hip hop beats—typically with a more modern pop touch—started to make the G-Funk sound of Dr. Dre—and many other rap production styles—feel derivative and old-fashioned, particularly as newer and sharper electronic sounds were being produced.

Thankfully, some groups were able to adjust their music to avoid becoming irrelevant. For example, Outkast saw their southern rap style—which used live instrumentation and a funkier sound than many of their contemporaries—get taken over by less talented groups who merely wanted to emulate Outkast's style.

Childish Gambino's 2018 hit "This Is America" addressed the problem of gun violence. The song was the rapper's first #1 hit on Billboard's Hot 100 chart, and won four Grammy Awards in 2019.

As a result, their fourth album, *Stankonia*, utilized a broader array of sounds—including electronic production, soul, and pop—to create an influential album that revitalized their popularity.

Years later, they were able to stay relevant by integrating even more old-school soul into their sound while upgrading their production to include even more synthetic elements. Jazz and classical music also made their way into Outkast's sound booth, which helped them weather the commercial downgrade that rap briefly suffered during the mid-2000s.

In many ways, this period could be considered the nadir of the genre both commercially and critically. While earlier rap music may not have sold as many copies as artists did even during this time, sales numbers sharply declined from previous years as the quality of the music arguably worsened. For example, mainstream rap started to fall into a trend known as crunk, a style inspired by southern rap that took out the instrumental diversity of the genre and replaced it with simple melodies, repetitive hooks, and basic rapping that focused mostly on bragging.

Popular crunk artists included Lil John, the Ying Yang Twins, and D4L. These groups all had big hits on the charts, but hardcore hip hop fans didn't take their music too seriously. Mostly, these artists were considered pop novelties who played basic songs that were easy to remember but hard not to forget once the song was over. And fans reacted by buying fewer albums, though the rise of digital piracy likely had a lot to do with this fall in sales.

However, rappers like Jay-Z remained an essential stabilizing element in the genre by staying both commercially and critically relevant. He, in particular, was able to bring a sense of style and class to the genre by changing up his approach on nearly every album and moving from musician to **entrepreneur** and businessman. And his lyrics—which remained dazzlingly complex—continued to focus on his life and the plight of the African-American in unique ways.

The previously mentioned Outkast also helped keep rap from

Award-winning R&B singer Toni Braxton has had a long and successful career. She has won nine Billboard *Music Awards and seven Grammy Awards, as well as many other accomplishments.*

becoming too simplistic during this time. And Kanye West—who started and will likely end his career as a controversial figure— brought in a new sense of production excellence to the genre and a willingness to experiment. Like Jay-Z, he changed up his approach on every album and brought something new with every release.

And, on a smaller but still substantial scale, rappers such as MIA, The Roots, Gnarls Barkley, and Mos Def helped to weather the crunk storm. This issue became even more prominent as snap music and, later, Soundcloud rap, became popular. These genres featured loud and aggressive arrangements but

R&B, Soul, and Gospel

were often simpler even than the more basic crunk style. And while these approaches have their fans, others were less than impressed. "Those college kids are tired of the [dumb] rap, the druggie rap, the future rap," notes rap producer Sickamore. "They're gonna want something else. They're gonna want somebody with a lot of substance."

Future Possibilities for R&B and Soul Music

Both R&B and soul music have weathered peaks and valleys in popularity, constant changes in style and instrumentation, and many other challenges to remain relevant and vital almost 100 years after their initial debut. The passion and energy that goes into these recordings help to fuel some of the best music of the time and keeps fans and artists working hard to stay relevant and engaging.

The future of the genres could go in any number of directions. The late 2010s see most of the negative trends from the mid-2000s corrected. British soul and contemporary R&B are very popular, and rap remains a strong genre for young fans who want music with a slightly harder edge. Breakthroughs in production continue to be implemented throughout each style.

For example, electronic music and full programming-based production get smoother and more fluent every year and—in the hands of a skilled producer—may sound almost as authentic as a live band performance. This trend is likely to continue into the future, though retro-oriented R&B may also remain a persistent interest for many fans.

As always, the cyclical nature of the music industry is likely to end genres when they've become stale and help kickstart new styles when they become necessary. The possibilities could be endless and are likely limited only by the imagination of future musicians and producers.

TEXT-DEPENDENT QUESTIONS

1. What artist was arguably the most popular female singer in British soul?

2. Which critic said that contemporary R&B was all about sound rather than songs?

3. Why did rap suffer a brief decline in sales in the mid-2000s?

RESEARCH PROJECT

Download a free trial version of a music making program, like Fruity Loops, and experiment with making beats and grooves. Try to emulate traditional R&B, soul, and rap sounds that you've heard in the past and compare them to other musicians. If you don't feel comfortable performing this task, download a few examples that you can examine to get an idea of how producers and songwriters create grooves.

CHAPTER NOTES

CHAPTER ONE

p. 8: "Gospel Music is a shining beacon…" Gospel Music Heritage Month Foundation, "A History of Gospel Music" (accessed April 2019). http://gospelmusicheritage.org/site/history/

p. 11: "Gospel music first emerged…" Teach Rock, "Gospel Music and the Birth of Soul" (accessed April 2019). https://teachrock.org/lesson/gospel-music-and-the-birth-of-soul/

p. 19: "Over the next few decades…" Paul McGuinness, "Change Is Gonna Come: How Gospel Influenced Rhythm'n'Blues," U Discover Music (August 26, 2018). https://www.udiscovermusic.com/in-depth-features/gospel-influenced-rhythm-n-blues/

CHAPTER TWO

p. 26: "The music was very instrumental…" Syl Johnson, quoted in Chris Jordan, "Struggle for Equality Was Set to Music," *USA Today* (February 25, 2014). https://www.usatoday.com/story/life/music/2014/02/25/black-history-civil-rights-music/5815065/

p. 29: "Brown had both the message…" Henry Adaso, "How James Brown Influenced Hip-Hop," Thought Co. (March 8, 2019). https://www.thoughtco.com/how-james-brown-influenced-hip-hop-2857334

p. 34: "Morton learned to play piano…" Biography.com Editors, "Jelly Roll Morton Biography," (accessed April 2019). https://www.biography.com/people/jelly-roll-morton-9415945

CHAPTER FOUR

p. 65: "Neo-soul, and some would…" Marcus Shepard, "Revisiting Neo-Soul," Confessions of an Aca-Fan blog (October 16, 2013). http://henryjenkins.org/blog/2013/10/revisiting-neo-soul.html

CHAPTER FIVE

p. 77: "Modern R&B isn't about discrete songs…" Robert Christgau, *Is It Still Good to Ya? Fifty Years of Rock Criticism, 1967–2017*. Durham, N.C.: Duke University Press, 2018.

p. 83: "Those college kids are tired…" Sickamore, quoted in Shawn Setaro, "What's Next in Rap?" Complex (January 16, 2018). https://www.complex.com/music/2018/01/what-experts-think-is-next-for-rap

A&R department—the talent department at a record label, which is responsible for finding artists and acquiring songs for them to record. A&R stands for "artists and repertoire."

audio mixing—the process by which multiple sounds are combined into a finished song. The music producer often uses a mixing console to manipulate or enhance each source sound's volume and dynamics.

ballad—a folk song that narrates a story in short stanzas.

beat—the steady pulse that listeners feel in a musical piece.

bootleg—an unauthorized recording of a song.

chord—three or more tones played at the same time.

copyright—the exclusive legal right to control the publication or reproduction of artistic works, such as songs, books, or movies. Musicians protect their original songs through copyright to prevent other people from stealing their songs, lyrics, or musical tunes. The period of copyright protection is generally seventy years after the death of the creator of the work.

demo—short for "demonstration recording," a song that that is professionally produced and recorded to demonstrate the ability of a musician or musical group.

harmony—the simultaneous combination of tones or pitches, especially when blended into chords that are pleasing to the ear.

hook—the "catchy" part of a song that makes people want to hear it repeatedly. The hook can be lyrical or musical. It is often the title of the song, and is usually repeated frequently throughout the song.

hymn—a song of religious worship.

instrumentation—the way a song's composer or arranger assigns elements of the music to specific instruments. When done for an orchestra, this is called "orchestration."

lyrics—the words of a song.

mastering—the final process of preparing a mixed recording for commercial distribution.

measure—a way of organizing music according to its rhythmic structure. Each measure, or "bar," includes a certain number of beats.

pitch—term used to describe how high or low a note sounds. Pitch is determined by the note's frequency, or the number of complete oscillations per second of energy as sound in the form of sound-waves.

producer—the person in charge of making a record. Chooses the musicians, instrumentation, and songs for the project, and oversees it to completion, often in collaboration with the recording artist and staff of the record company.

riff—a short repeated phrase in popular music and jazz, typically used as an introduction or refrain in a song.

rhythm—a strong, regular, repeated pattern of musical sounds.

scale—a sequence of notes in either descending or ascending order.

signature song—a song that a popular music artist or band is most known for or associated with, usually one of their biggest hits. The most popular artists can have more than one signature song.

solo—a piece of music, or a passage in a piece of music, that is performed by one musician.

tempo—the speed at which a piece of music is played.

1800s: The popularity of music among African-American slaves, such as spirituals and work songs, starts the early roots of gospel music.

1920s: The invention and popularization of in-home radios and record players help to bring gospel music to a broader music audience and inspires artists to streamline their styles into more secular forms. Thus, R&B and soul are eventually born.

1954: Ray Charles releases several gospel-fueled classics, including "I've Got a Woman," to inspire the early formation of soul music. Charles later fused country music with his sound to increase the range of soul even further.

1956: Elvis Presley records a version of Big Mama Thornton's hit "Hound Dog" that goes on to sell over 20 million copies.

1957: Stax Records forms and will put out some of the most influential and essential soul classics of all time. Their organ, guitar, and bass sound is often enhanced with horns and skilled vocalists paired with skilled songwriting and arranging by Isaac Hayes.

1959: Motown Records forms and puts out pop-styled soul and R&B music that helps to make African-American music more popular. R&B artists like Marvin Gaye, Stevie Wonder, and Michael Jackson get their start at Motown.

1961: Ben E. King's gospel-inspired soul classic "Stand By Me" becomes a huge crossover success, paving the way for increased acceptance of soul music.

1964: The Rolling Stones, an all-white British band, take on the style and sound of R&B and soul and transform it into a more rock-styled genre. This act brings about accusations of cultural appropriation, but also helps to spread the popularity of these styles.

1967: English R&B bands like the Rolling Stones and Small Faces embrace psychedelic music and inspire African-American performers like Sly and the Family Stone to follow suit. As a result, bands like Parliament and Funkadelic integrate more complex and rock-oriented styles into their music.

1967: James Brown hardens his sound, simplifies the melodies, and creates a new genre: funk. "Cold Sweat," released in this year, is considered the first funk song.

1970s: Disco and funk take the innovations of R&B and make them more suitable for dancing, once again expanding their influence. Though these styles eventually become outdated, new artists take over and help to keep the styles changing.

1980s: Quiet storm emerges as a popular new form of soul music that appeals to both black and white audiences. Rap music becomes a popular R&B alternative for younger listeners, tapping into their youthful angst and inspiring new variations on the sound, including the use of live instrumentation and sample-based production.

1990: Mariah Carey's debut single, "Vision of Love," helps to make contemporary R&B one of the most popular styles of music and brought the use of melisma (extended pitch variations while singing) into mainstream music.

1992: The surprise massive success of Whitney Houston's soundtrack for *The Bodyguard*, which sells 40 million copies, cements the popularity of contemporary R&B during this period and throughout much of the rest of the 1990s.

1992: Dr. Dre releases his solo debut *The Chronic*, which utilizes live instrumentation and organic sounds to increase the connection between rap and R&B. This style, known as G-Funk, becomes the dominant production style of rap for nearly a decade.

1995: D'Angelo's debut album *Brown Sugar* helps to kickstart the neo-soul genre, an off-shoot that recaptures some energy from the low-key quiet storm movement. His success inspires others, like Lauryn Hill and Erykah Badu, to explore soul and R&B more fully.

2000: Rap group Outkast release their eclectic masterpiece *Stankonia*, utilizing soul, electronic, and R&B elements to make the form more organic again. Later, the group would integrate jazz into their sound to make rap even more inclusive.

2003: Joss Stone's debut *The Soul Sessions* helps introduce British soul to a wider audience and begins a rejuvenation of the genre. Her collaborations with other artists also help to bring a wider range of acceptance for the form.

2006: Amy Winehouse's blockbuster second album *Back to Black*, brings tortured energy back into R&B and soul and utilizes classic R&B and soul styles. Her unfortunate early death inspires other female singers to emulate her style but not her life.

2011: Adele's second album 21 synthesizes classic soul and R&B sound with modern production to create classy pop music: it sells millions of copies. She remains one of the most popular recording artists of her generation.

2013: Robin Thicke's hit single "Blurred Lines" blends soul music and controversial lyrics about a sexual encounter.

2015: Alabama Shakes album *Sound and Color* showcases a very authentic form of soul that makes them one of the most talked about bands of the decade.

2018: Toni Braxton''s album *Sex and Cigarettes* earns a Grammy nomination for best R&B album.

Cosgrove, Stuart. *Detroit 67: The Year That Changed Soul.* New York: Clayton Publishing Group, 2015.

Darden, Robert. *People Get Ready!: A New History of Black Gospel Music.* New York: Continuum, 2005.

Mayfield, Todd, and Travis Atria. *Traveling Soul: The Life of Curtis Mayfield.* Chicago: Chicago Review Press, 2016.

Othello, Jeffery. *The Soul of Rock 'N Roll: A History of African Americans in Rock Music.* San Francisco: BookBaby, 2012.

Sullivan, James. *The Hardest Working Man: How James Brown Saved the Soul of America.* New York: Avery, 2008.

INTERNET RESOURCES

https://www.press.umich.edu/pdf/9780472071081-ch1.pdf
This in-depth examination of soul music helps track the changes in the genre and provides an even better understanding of the form.

https://firescholars.seu.edu/cgi/viewcontent cgi?article=1072 &context=honors
A study of the differences between various types of music, including R&B, and how they differ based on their uses of harmonies.

https://study.com/academy/lesson/rap-music-structure-techniques-tips.html
This detailed musical examination takes a look at how rap music is structured and the musical elements utilized in various styles.

https://study.com/academy/lesson/what-is-gospel-music-definition-history-artists.html
A lengthy look at gospel music and the influence it has had on popular culture.

http://www.newworldencyclopedia.org/entry/Gospel_music
An in-depth examination of gospel music and how it has changed over the years.

INDEX

AUTHOR'S BIOGRAPHY

ERIC BENAC is a hard-working freelance writer who has written several books for Mason Crest. He is also currently finishing up a collection of reviews on Frank Zappa and a few novels. In his spare time, he enjoys listening to and writing music, reading, hiking, swimming, and traveling.

CREDITS